Stirrup Your Faith
By Cassie Groff
AF593114
Receiving God's Love Through Horses

ISBN# 979-8353495185

Don't' be cheap, buy another copy.

Editor—Cindy K Roberts

Published in the United States of America

By Every Cowgirl's Dream

Cover design by Cindy K Roberts

Dedication

I dedicate this book to those that are struggling in their own lives. And I hope, by sharing my experiences with you, I can help you in some way, by pointing you in the right direction.

~Cassie Groff

Disclaimer

Testimony and experiences shared by the author may be coincidental to the reader. The names have been changed to protect the innocent .

Table of Contents

YOU ARE MY
FORTRESS, MY
REFUGE IN
TIMES OF
trouble

PSALM 59:16

Chapter 1

This is Me

For those who do not know me my name is Cassie. I got my first horse on my 12th birthday and because of her I am who I am today. God knew what I needed and kept me from going down a bad path.

I have moved around a lot! I was born in Evanston, Wyoming and lived several places in Colorado, before moving to Athol, Idaho for 4 years. My family moved to Kansas in 1995 and I've lived within 50 miles of the Redfield area ever since.

I have three teenage boys and have been through three marriages.

I love equines and try to help those that are in bad situations because they have no voice for themselves.; I've always had little confidence or trust in people and have always done better with animals.

When helping others with their horse's behavioral issues, most people chose not to learn or admit that they needed the help. The excuses I heard were that all the problems were the equine's fault, or they came just to ride or to get around my boys. That was when, I told myself I would not do lessons or any training for people again.

Then, one day I was asked by a parent to give lessons to

their kids. As I stated earlier, I did not want to do this again. I hesitated, drug my feet, and refused for probably a year or so. One day I really felt God starting to put pressure on me to do this, but I kept ignoring it. God didn't let up though, and I finally decided to do it, and because God asked me to do this, I decided to not get upset if they did not want to open their minds. I would simply plant a seed and let them decide whether it would grow or if it would stay dormant.

I realized that this is how I often responded when God asked me to do something. I would often let the seed He planted lay dormant rather than nurturing it. Thankfully, He has always been patient with me, and given me time to figure things out.

Those that have met me and share my life with me, know that my group has grown and I started feeling that God was wanting me to branch out; I then started teaching how I learned about patience, trust, pride and many other things, through the many equines I've interacted with. Now I am facing another big change in my life! I feel that God is asking me to branch out and help others. I would like to use my testimony and the many things I learned through equines, to shine God's light, and hopefully plant some seeds that will help others find or grow in the Lord.

Today will only be one account from the many lessons and experiences I've had, and later in the book, I will explain the rest of my testimony. Now you will hear about when I learned to trust God wholeheartedly. The kind of trust that removes anxiety, fear and worry.

Chapter 2

Let's Begin!

I have a question for all of you. How many of you take the time to watch people?

As a test, I will ask you, if you had the opportunity to meet me, what do you see when you look at me? What personalities, characteristics, or emotions do you feel? Some of you have openly told me your answers, yet I'd guess that most of you probably see just an ordinary, everyday kind of girl. I hope you see that I have found joy, and everything I need in God. Some things you may have noticed are:

My Smile

Some have said that my smile is this first thing they noticed. A smile usually represents happiness and joy. I can say I have my smile because of God's mercy and love for me. God also provided the funds for my parents to get me braces, to give me the smile I have. I'll explain more about my smile in the 2nd part of my testimony.

My Positive Outlook

Some have said that my positive outlook is what they noticed about me. I try to be positive, because I know God has control over everything, and I trust him.

My Desire to Help Others

Some have said, my desire to help others is what they noticed. I want to help others, because I'd like to use all the Lord has given me to help others.

The Care I Show Towards Others Who Are in Pain

The pain I went through makes me want to help others to

never have to feel the same pain like I did. I'd like to help those in pain or troublesome times so they feel better and are able to find true joy and happiness in Christ!

Because of the experiences and struggles in my life I have learned how to pay attention to people and animals.

I know how to see past the invisible mask that you put on; trying not to draw attention to yourself or let people know that you have problems.

I will also say that many people I know, may not have seen me as a person that is broken, untrusting, fearful, and full of sorrow and anger. Some may guess that my choice of relationships and divorces is the main cause for my pain and fear. At a different time, I hope to share with you most of my hidden secrets of pain, shame and fear... perhaps later.

If we have met in person, and you had known these things, would you look at me differently?

At five to six years of age, I learned how to hide my true feelings, and not draw unwanted questioning and attention to myself. Because of this, and the experiences and struggles I've had in my life, I have learned how to pay attention to people and animals. I know how to see past the invisible mask that many people put on...trying not to draw attention to themselves or let people know that they do have problems.

Behind each face, every person is hiding a struggle of their very own. Most of the people who are really struggling will never announce their pain, because they are ashamed of their past or are afraid of being judged.

As I've mentioned to you, behind my smile is a very broken, sad and hurting person. At times I have been envious of others because I believe, they've had a more normal, not so traumatic and pain filled life as I have.

At one of the women's bible studies, we studied the book of Esther, and one of the ladies mentioned that this book was an account of her personal life. Kind of like a diary account in a way.

We discussed how they prepared the women of that time for the king, to choose his new wife and what their life would be like afterwards, if they were not chosen. Probably not something most people would tell their friends or even strangers, yet it was recorded in the Bible for all of us to read. As we studied this, I realized that my life is not to different from hers. I felt God telling me that my negative experiences can develop into being a good thing if I shared my story with others; along with the positive thought to help others with their own struggles, like Esther did in the Bible.

I do not want to look at my past and hurt anymore. I want to look at how my past will help others people find Christ; and joy in all the storms they face in life. I chose to let my smile be a light to shine for God.

This is only a small introduction to my own testimony, if you want to hear the rest, keep reading. Thank you all for walking into my life; your being here will help me face my fears head on. I will ask you of one thing. PLEASE reach out to me and give me feedback. My desire is, for you to appreciate my efforts by my sharing my story with others. I will also say, I am not seeking anything by giving my testimony. I am sharing my testimony because, over the years, there have been special people who have touched my life and helped me see God's mercy. I would not change anything in my life, because it has made me who I am and it helped me to find true joy and happiness in God. I know that I am not an accident. I have a purpose and everything I have experienced has a purpose in God's perfect plan. And, he is not done refining me.

I have taken my experience and tried my hardest to help those that are struggling. To be honest, I have been back and forth on whether I wanted to do this since I am still alive and so are the people, connected in my testimony. So, if you know any of the people in my testimony, *PLEASE* do not be harsh on them! I have forgiven them, and love each and every one of them because without them, I could not possibly do what I am doing right now. As I have said multiple times, everything works towards God's plan!

Chapter 3

Trust

Just like humans horses are social creatures and they often display similar traits. A few are: patience, pride, and trust. Today I will briefly demonstrate trust. Pictured right is a horse named Star, I have owned her since she was 1.5 years old. I got her from a ranch that has around twenty foals a year. The foals do not get gentled or messed with until they are weaned and branded. Talk about a traumatic first handling! The second time they are handled, usually consists of being herded into a small pen, and singled out into a corner where they get their first halter forced onto them. This is not a cruel act, just a rushed one. Another common technique is roping them and putting the halter on them. So, their first experience with humans is not the greatest because they are scared.

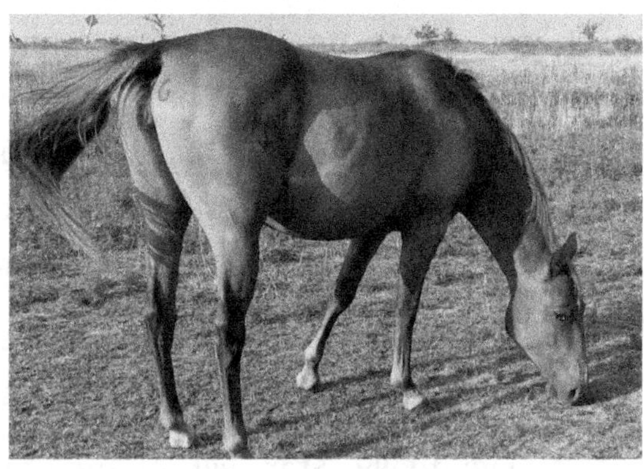

Horses are a flight animal because they are prey animals. So, when in danger they run!

Back to Star. Sadly I have not spent a whole lot of time with her, and it shows. She has not yet learned to fully trust me. This mule is named Spotless Prince. He

Spotless Prince with an admirer.

was the same way and as you see I do not have any problems touching him at all. He has learned to trust me, just as I've learned to trust God.

However, their situations are different just like they can be with you and me. Spotless Prince has had human contact since birth and I do not believe in forcing things on my equines (although if I'm pressed for time I often fall back to my old ways of training.) Unless it is a life or death situation, I try to guide them and let them make the decision rather than forcing things on them. **Just as God is with us, or as parents do with their children.**

So just like Star, I do not trust easily, and I used to try to control my life because I did not fully trust God with my life.

Eventually, Star will let me catch her, and if I were to continue this she would eventually be like Spotless and "catch me." I will try to catch her in the pasture and will not succeed. I will use grain to lure her into the round pen. After getting her in the pen you can see the steps I am using to help her see I am not going to hurt her. I want her to see that me touching her will not harm her but make her life better. If she trusts me enough to let me touch and catch her, it could save her life if she were injured. If she doesn't trust me, it could endanger her life even more! On the good side of things if she lets me catch and touch her, I can scratch her itchy spots, or take her in the yard to eat grass as a reward.

I will make mistakes and occasionally lose my temper, but if we develop a good enough relationship we can work together. My trust with people is a lot like a horse's trust in us often they trust us but are still cautious just as I have learned to trust but am still cautious.

For a long time, my trust of God was the same as my trust

in people, I was cautious and didn't fully trust Him. I blamed God for a lot of things in my life.

On March 9, 2011, my outlook on life and relationship with God changed!

It started out with, I had a rough year. I'd been taken to court by the state over child support issues, which then turned into a custody battle with my ex-husband. I had a six inch plus stack of false abuse charges filed against me. My parents were thinking about selling their house, and there was a possibility I could become homeless. I had people close by, but no one to go to. Due to all that, my relationship with my ex who was struggling...I was STRUGGLING!!!

After getting off work on March 9th, I stopped by my ex-husband's house for a little bit.

I got in my truck and went to pick up my boys from the bus stop. I remember, I was overcome with fear of losing everything I had and destroying other people's lives! I was crying angrily and started asking God to just take me! I didn't understand why I was even born! It seemed like everywhere I went I destroyed things or was not wanted. I felt like, I was a burden to everyone.

Next, I turned onto a limestone road and a teenage boy that had been [driving] in front of me on Locust ran a stop sign and t-boned my truck which caused me to slide! My truck then rolled, and it seemed like it went on forever! In that moment, the key points of my life flashed right before eyes! I did not have my seat belt on, and my truck was full of many hazardous deadly objects including: my boys three car seats in the back seat, a shovel, and three and a half ton floor jack that was under the back seat; including my purse and all my other personal belongings, and a Bible. The bed of my truck had hedge logs that were bigger than my arm (relevance to childhood wreck) and two spare tires! So, if you get the picture. The many dangerous objects flying through the air, or rolling, could have severely hurt or even killed me! I had no cuts, just an invisible but very painful bruise where my seatbelt should have been!

Through all this mess, I know God was there, because the only thing left in the whole truck was my Bible and myself!!!!!! I said earlier, while my truck was rolling and tumbling over and over, it seemed like my life flashed before me! I remember thinking about everything! I then realized my life resembled, my truck rolling from one disaster to another. To get a picture of what the scene looked like, I had let go of the steering wheel, and planted my arms against the ceiling; with my feet on the floor, holding on for dear life. I then remember, asking God to take me from this world! The answer came loud and clear to me. His answer was NO! He was NOT done with me yet!

I decided at that moment to stop trying to control my life and let go of the reins. I then told God he could have the reins; I was tired of failing. My truck then stopped rolling!

After the shock wore off, I made sure someone was picking up my boys from the bus. I then started picking up my things out of the road and ditch. That is when I realized that the Bible was the only thing left in the truck. I knew right then that God was there the entire time the Bible just confirmed it for me!

As I sat next to my truck crying, I thanked God for saving me and giving me more time with my boys. I also asked forgiveness for not thinking of God or anyone else. At that point in my life, I stopped worrying about tomorrow and found joy in every moment of my life from that moment on.

To be honest, this was not the only time in my life that I had asked God to take me. Many times, while riding in a vehicle with an abusive person I wanted to throw myself from the vehicle! The person who I loved, was not home with me and was being unfaithful. [Often] I was home alone and thought of taking my life with a gun! I even got to the point of holding the gun in my hands!

This very accident scared me the most because:

1. I did not have control over if I would live or die.
2. And, I had just asked God to take me.

I often wondered, if I would ever run out of tears and asked how much more pain can I possibly endure? When would it be my turn to find joy and happiness?

During the accident, while rolling in my truck, I realized all I needed to do was look to God for joy, and he immediately answered!

This very accident helped me to find joy. Not in people, but in God! It helped me to trust him and that took away all my anxiety, fears and "what if's." God brought me peace.

This is just one story of me learning to trust God with my life. And just like Star, I have other stories that can show you the many steps God has used to guide and direct me. The steps it took to get me to trust him whole heartedly through all storms. To be able to find joy in all situations.

I wish I could say that you have heard the hardest times in my life, however my struggles started at age 5-6 years old. So, I will not be able to go into all of it now. More on that later.

Again, I ask you not to give me sympathy. I want you to see that God is the light in my suffering.

I have been blessed to have a mother always searching God's word and giving me spiritual advice. I also have an amazing God who never gives up on me and always saw me as something valuable instead of a lost cause or something worthless. God gave me my first horse to become my best friend and I'm so thankful for that! Without her, I would have gone down a bad path in my life.

I hope through my testimony that you can look past the things you see, and reach out as a Christian to listen and witness to others. People do not realize that it is the small things that make a difference in other people's lives. Taking the time to think of others and sometimes becoming selfless can change your life and theirs. If someone would have reached out to me and made me feel like I was not a mistake, I may not have gone through so many hardships.

So, make those phone calls, send those text messages, or just stop by and visit someone. It could change their life!!!

Chapter 4

How I Became Who I Am

For the story of how I became who I am. How I learned to become independent, strong and the stages of trusting and accepting God. As told earlier, we moved around quite a lot, I experienced intimidating events in my life; I am sure I am not aware of everything due to God's amazing gift of forgetting traumatic and painful memories. I was told by my mom that I went to a horse Bible camp where the counselor told my mom, I stayed to myself and didn't have much to do with the horses. For those who know me I'm sure you're thinking WHAT? Negative incidents are the very start of learning how to put on a mask.

In my personal life, because my mom could see the pain, shame and fear on the outside; she started asking questions. Between the fear of caving and telling her about this negative experience, every time she asked questions, it just made me hurt and feel worse. So, I chose to shut myself from the world and bury my past.

We moved to Gore mountain range in Colorado and it was then I felt a sense of peace. We had five acres of peace and tranquility. It was here that my mom and dad decided to start having us memorize Bible verses. Sometime before moving here, I accepted **Jesus** as my savior not understanding it just doing what others were doing to make my mom proud of me. But there was something with the first verse that hit me and is the sole reason for who I am.

Phil 4:13 [NIV] I can do all things though Christ who strengthens me.

Basically, I realized that with God I could get through anything. When I felt weak, I would say the verse and ask God to be with me and give me the strength to get though another hurdle. I knew nothing was impossible if I depended on God for strength.

I then continued to struggle at home and school. Feeling dirty, worthless, and angry. My 2nd grade teacher didn't help much, he had a reputation of flunking kids he didn't like; I was one of them. I would compare my assignments with other students, and he would mark my correct answers wrong and if I asked why, he would just yell at me. My mom tried to get involved, but it did no good. I then learned no matter what I did, and how hard I tried nothing would ever be good enough. So, I quit trying. It was easier to get in trouble for not doing something than putting all your efforts into it.

My next teacher was very understanding and helped me a lot to start trying again. This lasted for a while, then my life would change drastically again. My dad's job would change due to the lumber plant closing. He got transferred to Athol, Idaho. He decided to keep us out of school for a bit to help us get adjusted then we went to school with little time left. Hurt, due to being taken from my friends and everything I knew, and losing time to do schoolwork; my grades declined. I ended up with a D in math, so my parents decided to hold me back. And I just made new friends!

Now I would have to make new friends in a different grade. The good part was this, I didn't have to face all my classmates that I used to be with the year before, because my parents [then] realized that we were in the right school district. So, I'm staying in the same grade and changing schools for now. I then rebelled against my parents and with school; but school came easy, so I didn't suffer much. I just didn't do my homework.

I regret it today because, if I had tried, where could I be now? I didn't hurt my parents...I hurt myself. It was here, that God gave me the best thing to help me through [all of this] all my past and future...my first horse, and best friend, Sundance.

I was never accepted by people; I don't know if it was my looks or my personality. The reason Sundance was my best friend, is because, I had no one that I could say were true friends. The people I hung out with at home said we couldn't be friends in public; and I only talked with teachers at school.

In the first of my testimony, I mentioned if you physically met me, you might remark that what you liked about me, was my smile. At this time, I had crooked teeth and an overbite; which is why I said it could've been my looks that was the reason I had no friends. It wasn't all bad there though, we started in a little church which broke up, and my dad helped start a new one. It was cool seeing my dad doing sermons and they had a really good teen program. It was through the teen program that I accepted Christ as my savior at a teen event in Washington. We went to a Christian concert which I wasn't really impressed with, but it was a cool experience. Afterwards, we went to a place where a college group of kids were putting on their own concert; it was one of the songs that really touched me. The girls singing in it came over to me and helped me to ask Jesus into my life. For the first time in my life I felt a release like I wasn't alone anymore. I knew God he gave me strength but now I knew, he dwelt in me and I was never alone.

John 3:16 [NIV] For God so loved the world that he gave his one and only Son, that whoever believes in him shall not perish but have eternal life.

I still struggled with self-worth though, and I started getting responsibilities of babysitting; I was often wrongfully accused of things by my siblings or neighbors, and occasionally my parents. To rectify this, I tried so hard to make people happy.

I liked seeing smiles on people's faces because it made me feel better; I was so hurt inside. If I could make someone else feel better, it made me feel better about myself because I made one person not live in sorrow or pain. I knew, I didn't want anyone to live the way I did. I continued to not put all my efforts forward, because no matter how hard I tried, I got in trouble.

I remember a day when something happened, and I was so happy, because I wasn't the only one who got in trouble for something I didn't do. Mom lined us all up and asked us [who did it] and no one admitted so then, we all got a spanking. I remember the happiness I felt because even though I got hurt for something I didn't do, the others did and so did the culprit. Recently, we found out it might have been none of us, and may have been our neighbor. My siblings are still devastated by that event! I told them that was my daily life being punished for what they did, because I was the oldest!

So, to stay out of trouble I was either on my horse or on our mountain. I stayed away from my family as much as possible and away from people. I was becoming a teenager during this time period, and my interest in guys started growing and that is where my horse helped me a lot. My horse had most of my attention; without her, I'm not sure what I would have done! As Buck Brannaman said, "there are things that the horse did for me that a human couldn't have done."

Slowly my anger started growing from being rejected by people and being blamed for things I didn't do. I just wanted to feel a part of something and not feel like an outcast and a failure anymore. On one of the many fights, I had with my mom, she slapped me and told me, I was going to tell her what had happened to me in a town where we once lived.

With tears in my eyes I caved in, and told her everything. It was now at this point in my life,] I didn't feel the people from my past, could hurt me anymore. Because of my struggle, I couldn't hold it in any longer. I finally felt a release like a huge burden had been released from my soul! It was then, my mom told me to not let things bottle up inside me like this and to always give it to God and allow others to help me.

In Idaho, it was then my fresh start began with my relationship with God, and my start in the recovery and healing from my negative experiences. I learned to forgive those who do wrong to us, and not harbor hate towards others. I also learned that we are to love everyone, although I still had a long way to go with my inner growth and I didn't truthfully understand it.

I wish I could say at that moment, I lived a straight and Christian life; I still put my joy in people however, I wasn't giving God my whole life. I was still controlling most of my life.

We moved to Kansas where I am currently living. I was now 15 years old, in a new school again. This time a new high school where it is even harder to fit in and find friends. You are joining a group of people that have been together since they were young. Outsiders are not always welcome, the older you get. They will be nice to your face but not accept you or let you join in. It was at this time, my parents were able to get braces for me; maybe that is what changed as far as starting to be accepted.

We moved closer to our family in Kansas which might be good but didn't help me much, because I was always cast aside by all of them. I was never really liked, and it became more evident when I moved here. I was told many times, I wouldn't graduate from high school and that I would be pregnant before I graduated from high school.

My experiences over the years made me become stronger and even more strong-willed. If someone said I couldn't or wouldn't do something, I would work my hardest to prove them wrong!

My first boyfriend was when I was 15 years old and I thought I found everything! Love, happiness and acceptance! The relationship started going downhill because of my past; I didn't realize that the "if you love me" and him making me feel like I wasn't doing something right was the reason I would end up doing something that I knew was wrong. He also started leaving bruises on my arms from grabbing me.

I broke up with him and thought I did better, thinking I found someone who cared for me again. We were together for quite a few years; and I caught him cheating on me many of the years, but I was so scared of being alone! My thoughts were at least he wasn't pressuring or abusing me.

Later, I got married where more cheating occurred in my life, and looking back, I should've given it all to God, but that is my cross to bear. I divorced him. I tried really hard to find someone God fearing, and who would be a good role model for my son, when I remarried. As they say, when the honeymoon is over then the true person started revealing himself.

There are many reasons for masks to hide past experiences and to deceive people. I experienced both in my lifetime although I never tried to deceive people, I want everyone to know that I have a lot of baggage; I'm not perfect nor easy to deal with at times. It was then, my husband's past of drinking and drugs started to affect our relationship. Due to drinking, he would become very emotionally abusive from telling me, I was not a good mother or wife and I wasn't a good housekeeper. He would also get so drunk; while I was driving, he would attempt to grab the steering wheel and would say if 'I can't

have you no one could.' Never had I even hinted or thought of leaving him! It wasn't just me in the vehicle it was me, him, and my son, while I was pregnant with number two!

Also, while in my late pregnancy he went out with a friend and came back home really late...drunk. I had my window opened and I overheard them talking about him hitting on a high school girl and getting beat up by the boyfriend. He had a nasty, black eye. He told me once, I was really naive and he could cheat on me without even knowing. I knew, I just decided at that point, to let God help me with it. It was during this time, that I would have an extremely hard time dealing with an abusive relationship. There was no one to help me; in fear of my parents' opinion of him and his mother thinking I was just wanting to leave him. That I didn't love him, I shut myself in with my misery, and tried to rely on God for strength.

Deuteronomy 31:6 [NIV]

Be strong and courageous. Do not be afraid or terrified because of them, for the Lord your God goes with you; he will never leave you nor forsake you."

My parents ended up moving before my youngest son was born. During this hard time between my 2nd and youngest son's birth, dealing with a positive case of the first stages of cervical cancer, and afraid of becoming pregnant during this time, I started my shots of birth control again; which affected my hormones drastically. The doctor and myself were trying to find ways of dealing with the birth control side of things because my husband wasn't willing to wait till, we cleared everything. I insisted on protection.

One time, he was very drunk and insisted on no protection. I refused, he finally agreed; but honestly, he never intended on using protection at that time, and I became pregnant.

I didn't find out immediately that I was pregnant, it was during an ultrasound to get an understanding of my cancer that we found out I was pregnant, and the cancer was not present. God answered my prayer for the cancer and gave me a much greater gift!

2 Corinthians 9:15
Thanks be to God for his indescribable gift!

After having my youngest child and my parents being gone; things got worse. We were now at risk of losing our house due to his drinking, and not having enough money to pay the bills. I attempted to leave him, by going to my parents, where he threatened to burn down the house to get me back! I called the sheriff to help protect me; they told me they couldn't do anything. We ended up losing our house due to foreclosure, and then moved to Missouri. His drinking continued and the abuse wasn't getting any better.

Next, my husband started becoming abusive to my oldest son and I tried my very hardest to protect him. The drinking got heavier, and it started affecting us in the way of food. We didn't have much money for food, and he wouldn't let me shop for food unless it was the WIC I received. So, a lot of the times that's all me and the boys had. At that time, it was just beans, peanut butter, cereal, milk and bread. Sometimes, we would get steak or chicken when he was drunk, and he wanted to grill out...or when he wanted to go out to eat and drink.

It was then I learned to hide food from him, and I learned truthfully to trust God. At times when I didn't know how we would have food to eat, there was always some miracle that would make it possible for us to get food!

I then understood what it could've been like for the people fleeing Egypt, and it was God that provided manna and water for them daily.

Proverbs 3:5-6 [NIV]
Trust in the Lord with all your heart and lean not on your own understanding; in all your ways submit to him, and he will make your paths straight.

Matthew 6:26 [NIV] Look at the birds of the air; they do not sow or reap or store away in barns, and yet your heavenly Father feeds them. Are you not much more valuable than they?

Psalms 104:14 [NIV] He makes grass grow for the cattle,
and plants for people to cultivate—
bringing forth food from the earth:

Exodus 14:1-4 14 [NIV] Then the Lord said to Moses, 2 "Tell the Israelites to turn back and encamp near Pi Hahiroth, between Migdol and the sea. They are to encamp by the sea, directly opposite Baal Zephon. 3 Pharaoh will think, 'The Israelites are wandering around the land in confusion, hemmed in by the desert.' 4 And I will harden Pharaoh's heart, and he will pursue them. But I will gain glory for myself through Pharaoh and all his army, and the Egyptians will know that I am the Lord." So the Israelites did this.

5 When the king of Egypt was told that the people had fled, Pharaoh and his officials changed their minds about them and said, "What have we done? We have let the Israelites go and have lost their services!" 6 So he had his chariot made ready and took his army with him. 7 He took six hundred of the best chariots, along with all the other chariots of Egypt, with officers over all of them.

8 The Lord hardened the heart of Pharaoh king of Egypt, so that he pursued the Israelites, who were marching out boldly. 9 The Egyptians—all Pharaoh's horses and chariots, horsemen, and troops—pursued the Israelites and overtook them as they camped by the sea near Pi Hahiroth, opposite Baal Zephon.

10 As Pharaoh approached, the Israelites looked up, and there were the Egyptians, marching after them. They were terrified and cried out to the Lord. 11 They said to Moses, "Was it because there were no graves in Egypt that you brought us to the desert to die? What have you done to us by bringing us out of Egypt? 12 Didn't we say to you in Egypt, 'Leave us alone; let us serve the Egyptians'? It would have been better for us to serve the Egyptians than to die in the desert!"

13 Moses answered the people, "Do not be afraid. Stand firm and you will see the deliverance the Lord will bring you today. The Egyptians you see today you will never see again. 14 The Lord will fight for you; you need only to be still."

Chapter 5

Lessons Through More Hard Times

Then night came; he actually tried to hit me and I felt relieved. I told him I wished he would hit me; so that the pain would be evident. I knew that the bruising would go away a lot easier, than the scars left by his words. Sadly, he didn't hit me. It was also during this time in our marriage, when the presence of my parents visiting would be the hardest experience of my life. They didn't know what I was going through financially in acquiring food for my household; they came the day before that I would have money to buy food to entertain guests. So, the first night, I didn't have much. My dad said he was very disappointed that he raised a hostess like me; and that is how most of my parent's visits would go after that one experience, at any of the homes that I have lived.

That was another case of a mask I put on, and no one knew what I was dealing with; at that time in my life, I needed my families love and support more than ever. Just a simple hug, and I love you would have filled my soul with assurance. We ended up struggling financially again; and then my parents' house became open to us. We then moved back to my old house. I felt a bit of security because, I knew his drinking wouldn't make me homeless. I still hid food from him, due to the fact he didn't always make sure we had food, and when he drank, he would start snacking and eat everything in the house!

Next, we started counseling and he stopped drinking; and now he was working on his emotional abuse. Then he changed his tactics and started Bible shaming me! The preacher brought it to our attention, by announcing it during one of our sessions; when my husband started saying something about me. I then chose to divorce him, due to the abuse to my son and myself.

I did it in a way, that again helped me in my growth in God. I couldn't find a job to support myself, so I chose to go on assistance to escape him. I then lived on $600 a month for utilities, and living expenses. My utilities almost equaled that amount. I also had to make trips to Coffeyville to take Logan to his dad. God always provided ways to make things happen. Food was finally something that wasn't a fear with food stamps; I felt relieved that my kids could finally eat good healthy meals. God taught me to rely 100% on him. I didn't worry about money shelter or food anymore, because he was there for me.

Proverbs 3:5 [NIV] Trust in the Lord with all your heart and lean not on your own understanding;

I know there isn't a normal life; we all have our own struggles. I often get envious of those who have what I think would be considered a more normal life. Meaning, that they don't have to constantly be on guard of being hurt or losing something. I will explain further.

With divorce, comes a lot of struggles and fighting. I decided a long time before, I wouldn't drag the kids through a nasty divorce; all I wanted was for them to be safe. Due to greed or revenge, there were many accusations of abuse or neglect. So, everything I do has to be documented. I can never delete emails, texts or voicemails. I also documented everything prior to the divorces due to abuse and unfaithfulness. Sadly, divorce wasn't the only thing that caused difficulties in keeping my children. Envious or bitter people have made up stories, and tried to prove negligence or abuse. Sadly, in my possession, I have an over six inch stack of false charges on me; false charges of me tying my kids up, to feeding them cat food, and much more! I have lived in fear that I would lose my kids every day! I had to watch everything I have done with my kids; I had to listen to everyone judging me on how I have raised my kids! I was then aware that I never wanted my son to go through the same negative experiences in my life that I had to endure.

As you can see, my life has been filled with a lot of pain and sorrow, shame and guilt. A lot of "if you love me you will" ... and me just wanting to feel accepted and actually worth something. People used me, to get their own joy and pleasure. I felt I had been hurt deeply by people who were supposed to love you and protect you.

I searched so long for joy and happiness and God was with me the whole way if I would have looked for him and his unwavering love and he had already given it to me with my horse, Sundance and later, my three amazing boys. I had a mother who searched God's word and always gave me spiritual guidance and watching her go through her struggles gave me someone to look up to. In a way if I would've listened, I would've realized he was telling me not to look in people for joy and happiness it's just in him. God was always present in all of my situations helping me no

Proverbs 3: 6 [NIV] in all your ways submit to him, and he will make your paths straight. 7 Do not be wise in your own eyes; fear the Lord and shun evil.

matter if I knew it or not.

Even though I might have been mad at him because I didn't feel he was helping me. I learned not to trust people; only God. Now that doesn't mean that I treat people any differently. God gifted me with mercy and a want to help others. I look at Jesus' life and how he didn't change himself for others he still loved and respected them even though they hurt him. I try to be as loving and forgiving as him. I also know in some of my experiences I am just as guilty as those who have hurt me. So, I will not change myself. I will continue to help and be there for everyone no matter how they treat me. I will treat everyone how I want to be treated, and I will always attempt to notice those who appear to be struggling. I will offer my ears and time to those who need it. There is so much more of my life that has not been told and may never be expressed to anyone. For respect of those still being with us, I am not wanting them to be judged. This long bumpy road has taught me that God is my everything!

Do Not Worry

Mathew 6:25-26 [NIV] "Therefore I tell you, do not worry about your life, what you will eat or drink; or about your body, what you will wear. Is not life more than food, and the body more than clothes? 26 Look at the birds of the air; they do not sow or reap or store away in barns, and yet your heavenly Father feeds them. Are you not much more valuable than they?

Do Not Worry

Mathew 6:27-34 [NIV] "Can any one of you by worrying add a single hour to your life? And why do you worry about clothes? See how the flowers of the field grow. They do not labor or spin. 29 Yet I tell you that not even Solomon in all his splendor was dressed like one of these.

30 If that is how God clothes the grass of the field, which is here today and tomorrow is thrown into the fire, will he not much more clothe you—you of little faith? 31 So do not worry, saying, 'What shall we eat?' or 'What shall we drink?' or 'What shall we wear?'

32 For the pagans run after all these things, and your heavenly Father knows that you need them. 33 But seek first his kingdom and his righteousness, and all these things will be given to you as well. 34 Therefore do not worry about tomorrow, for tomorrow will worry about itself. Each day has enough trouble of its own.

I have learned that I need fellowship and family and I am called to love everyone. This has been hard for me because I have been hurt by so many people including those who are the closest and I had the most trust in. I just wanted to disappear or stay as far from people as possible. I realized, I am no better than those that have hurt me. I am a sinner, and have and continue to hurt people; I do not intentionally try to hurt people I am a sinner and will make mistakes. I try to ask myself, am I portraying a Godly person, and will I lead someone to God or not?

I have also tried to contact all those I have hurt in the past and ask for their forgiveness. I have so much more that I can add into my testimony but due to the length and time, I will stop here. This is things of my past that impacted my life tremendously.

You may think that what I'm telling you in this message is, I have everything figured out and I am always happy. That is not completely true! I have my daily struggles and am faced with my past experiences daily. These experiences haunt me all the time in every experience I encounter. I just learned to give it all to God, I wasn't supposed to do this on my own!

I give my worries, sorrows and needs to him! I have my low moments, but I know God has this! Instead of worrying, I go to prayer. Instead of fighting back I let God fight my battle. What can you get from my testimony? I hope you get that there are people out there that are hurting and longing for peace, joy and to be accepted.

- Do you pay attention enough to see through their masks?
- What have you done to show them about God?
- Are you being a Godly witness?
- What would Jesus do if he encountered someone struggling pass them by or offer an ear, shoulder or the truth that you always have someone with you through everything?

That's why I have taken my experiences and become selfless about my time and I listen when needed to offer my shoulder and all I know about God. I share my experiences to glorify him!

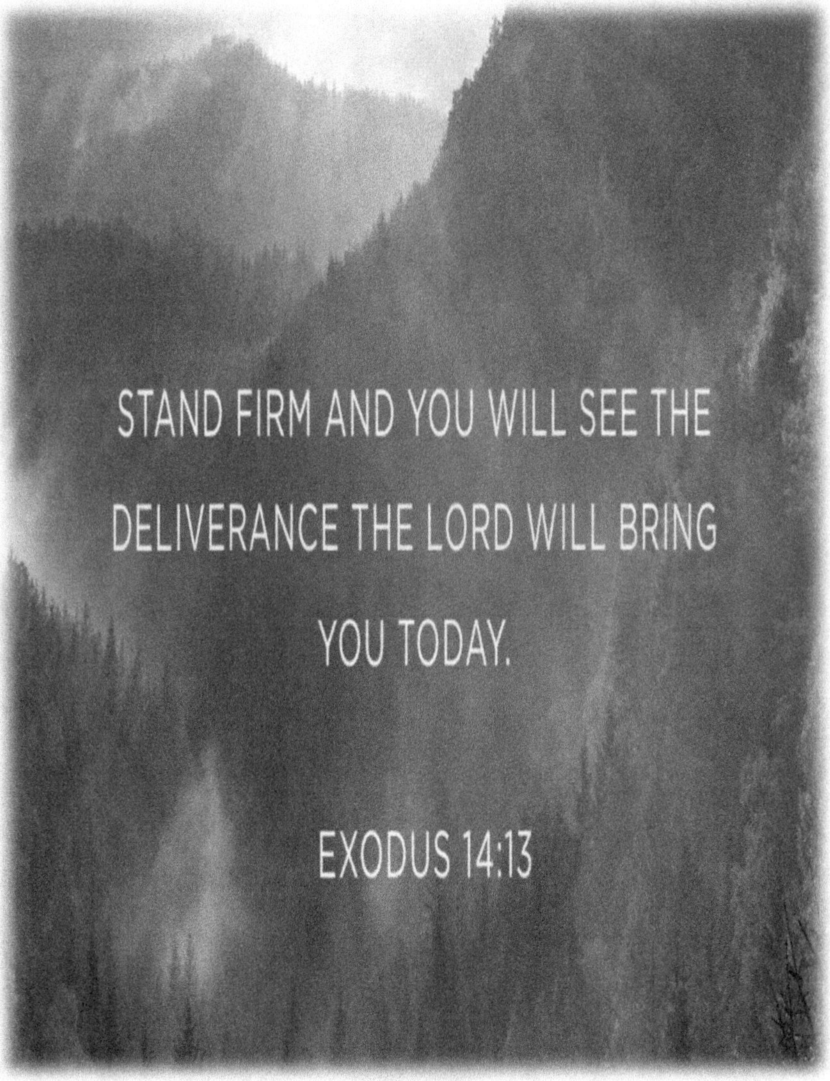

STAND FIRM AND YOU WILL SEE THE DELIVERANCE THE LORD WILL BRING YOU TODAY.

EXODUS 14:13

Chapter 6

Redemption Through The Trainer

The Seed Sown

People: Some people are born into a Christian family and go to church, and God's word stirs you and it is then, you ask him into your life. But for some, they are not born again or taught about God's love. So the seed planted in their hearts can be maybe a movie they watch, or going through a hardship, or someone talking to them about God; it could be through jail ministry, or someone teaching about equines and God's word together. Whatever the situation, once they hear or see it, this causes them to become curious and wanting to learn more, even if they don't want to accept or acknowledge it.

Equine: Some equines are born around people; and some have never been touched or had any sight of people. With the equines that have been around people, learning about the trainer is a little easier because they get training as they grow up, and want to please their trainer. For the equine that has not been around or touched by a person, its harder for them to accept them as a trainer or master. Much like us, they are born with curiosity.

For both, people and equines, learning to trust their master or God, learning to obey their master or God, learning to submit to their master or God, and accepting their trainer to be their master, or God to be our savior is very similar.

Isaiah 41:10 [NIV] So do not fear, for I am with you;
do not be dismayed, for I am your God.
I will strengthen you and help you;
I will uphold you with my righteous right hand.

Learning to Submit

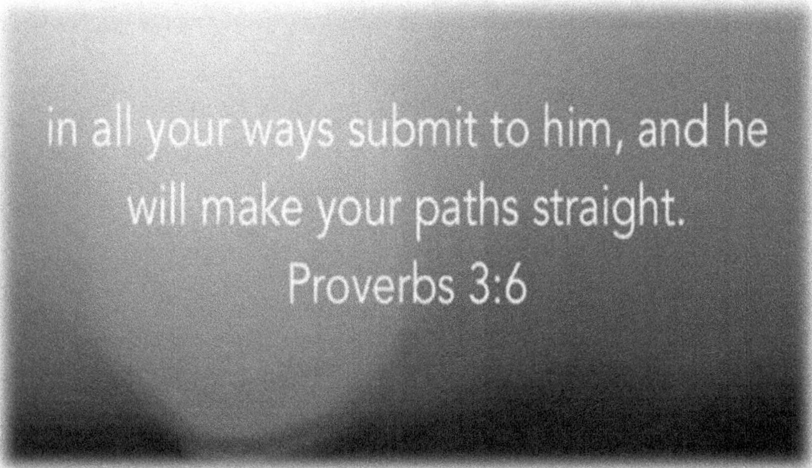

People: Our old self dies, we're born again but our old flesh is still sinful in nature. Learn to submit to God and obey his word. This is a daily task of reading his word and applying it to yourself. The flesh wants to do what it wants to without restrictions. The flesh wants to make its own decisions. We want to control our own lives. God lets us make mistakes and lets us learn from them; he is patient and merciful.

Equine: They try to assert their authority, testing their boundaries, they too are learning to submit to our training. Herd mentality naturally makes them want to dominate over their owner/trainer. To control the situation, if they have a good trainer, they will eventually learn to submit without force. A good trainer shows mercy and patience and allows them to learn at their own pace. A good trainer, lets them make mistakes so they can learn from them. When the submission is allowed from the equine to the good trainer, that is when there is a life long bond that forms.

For both groups, learning to submit is a lot of trial and error. It is death to the old self, and eliminating trying to control everything. It is seeking truths in the word or in the trainer.

Psalm 25:1 [NIV] In you, Lord my God, I put my trust.

Trusting the Trainer

People: During hard times we have to trust that God will never give us more than we can handle. We also have to learn to give our problems to God and trust he will take care of them for us.

We have to trust God's plan and path for us. Trust that he will never leave or forsake us.

Equine: Learning to trust that they will be safe. As we introduce every obstacle, animal or object; helping them to see that you will protect them. Trust will never be found in ways that they feel harmed or unsafe. They learn to trust your paths, your direction. They slowly trust their lives with you and trust you will never as them to do something that will harm both of you.

The Training Begins

People: When we start going to church, bible studies or searching his word or Christians to learn more this is when our life long training begins. Everyday refining us to become better Christians. Some of us learn by trial and error, by watching and learning from others and others learn by reading and applying it to their lives. Training begins when we accept God as our personal savior and when we decide to submit to him.

Equine: Whether it's the first time being haltered, asking the colt to lead; this foundation training and introduction to new things will be a life long process. It will be refining them into a trusting/working equine of whatever discipline that is being taught. They also learn by trial and error, by example or being led by the trainer. Training begins when the horse's curiosity stirs them to want to learn more from the trainer, and then accepts him or her as the leader of the herd.

For both, training is a life long process and always learning more to become better at what they do.

Author working with a colt named "Sport."

Mentorship

People: We all have that one person we look to for answers or one that we look up to. As we grow, we set a goal to witness or teach like the person we have looked up to. We learn respect, patience, study habits, praying and so much more through mentorship. Having someone to go to, or talk with, while you are growing is very important; especially during the hard times. Without a mentor, learning is harder emotionally and physically.

Equine: A seasoned equine can teach the younger green equine more than a human could every teach them. Not saying its impossible to teach them the trainer will just have to work harder to teach them. When a seasoned equine is present learning patience, cues, or respect comes easier and the equine is less stressed and remains calmer.

For both having a good mentor is very important for the personal training in their lives. Having someone to ask or lead causes less stress and less traumatic experiences. Because we are both social creatures going through things with others, makes learning easier especially from one has gone through similar training in their lives.

Stumbling blocks/right paths/influences

Psalms 1:1-6

Psalms 1: 1-2 [NIV] Blessed is the one
who does not walk in step with the wicked
or stand in the way that sinners take
or sit in the company of mockers,
2 but whose delight is in the law of the Lord,
and who meditates on his law day and night.

Psalms 1: 3-4 [NIV]

That person is like a tree planted by streams of water, which yields its fruit in season
and whose leaf does not wither—
whatever they do prospers.

4 Not so the wicked!
They are like chaff
that the wind blows away.

5 Therefore the wicked will not stand in the judgment, nor sinners in the assembly of the righteous.
6 For the Lord watches over the way of the righteous, but the way of the wicked leads to destruction.

People: Hanging out with friends that are not Christians could bring you down as a Christian. If witnessing, you need to be careful that you are not tempted to follow their paths to make you stumble in your walk with God. Sometimes the things you start doing are so small, that you don't even notice at first. We will make the mistake of following, and God patiently and kindly will redirect our paths. Sometimes we don't even have to have a person that can bring us down it can be things we watch on TV, things we do with our free time like games, sports, or hobbies. These can be stumbling blocks as well. Learning to identify them is crucial to your growth

Author, ponying a young horse.

Equine: Sometimes riding or leading your equine around with green or untouched equines it can cause them to become very unpredictable. They may spook or not listen when commands are given. They watch the behavior of the other equine and follow them. So making sure you have a good training foundation in them and a trust that has been established can help them to choose the right path of paying attention to you instead of the misbehaving equine. They are still a living thing and will stumble, so all we can do is patiently redirect them.

For both, choosing the correct person or truth to follow is very important. In both, a good trainer having patience and kindness to redirect the wrong decisions and God redirecting our path to help us for future decisions and experiences.

All the glory goes to God -The skill of the equine gives glory to the trainer.

We look to God for direction and the equine looks to the trainer for direction

Proverbs 3:6 In all thy ways acknowledge him, and he shall direct they paths.

The trainer rejoices when the equine does the correct thing when asked and God delights when we choose the correct paths.

Proverbs 23:16 Yea, my reins will rejoice, when thy lips speak the right things.

<u>Faith the Size of A Mustard Seed</u>

Faith in God, faith in the equine, faith in the trainer/rider

Faith through every experience on life, the good and bad.

- Do you have faith in God?
- Do you have faith in yourself?
- Do you have faith in your equine?
- Do others have faith in you?

Luke 17:6 And the Lord said if ye had the faith as a grain of mustard seed.

Equines will test our fear, patience, humility, meekness, laziness, trust, willingness, longsuffering and many others. How will you react? Can you identify the things you need to work on to make your relationships with people, God or your equine better?

Buck Brannaman says "The horse is a mirror to your soul. Sometimes you might not like what you see sometimes you will"

"I've always told people who ask, if there is a God: get around enough people with horses and see what happens. See how they survive in spite of all the things they do and you'll become a believer"

Chapter 7

Lessons Learned On The Back Of An Equine

Sense of accomplishment, strength to not give up.

My first horse was perfect for me; stubborn enough to make me work, but safe enough for a beginner. I love challenges and work better under finding solutions. One challenge was my height. I have always been short and if I wanted to ride, I had to rely at first on a parent to help me. After a while they got busy and I had to figure it out on my own. My horse wasn't very tall thank goodness, so it wasn't too hard. My mom taught me how to Indian mount a horse bareback and I started riding bareback more than with a saddle with me and I used his bike tire to jump on her. This did not end well I used to much force in the jump and went right over her back and on the ground onto the other side. Until I perfected that, I used things to jump on her back. One time my neighbor and riding his bicycle Where am I going with this I had always felt like I was incapable of doing anything right like a failure. I learned independence to saddle or mount bareback on my own. Now this does get me into trouble quite often riding when I wasn't supposed to. I also wanted the approval and wanted to be able to spend time with my parents so I started saddling 3 horses without knowing if they would go but if they were saddled most of the work was done already. Mom usually said yes and those were some of my best memories.

Watching an equine that I have solely worked with turning into a working equine gives me a sense of accomplishment. Its not just my accomplishment it's a team effort, it wouldn't be possible without the cooperation of the equine. So thankful God gave me the ability and skills to work with equines.

Acceptance

Due to my personality or looks, (which I do not know) I didn't have many friends. The ones that were my friends in Idaho, were only my friends at home and not allowed at school. I was always accepted by the horses I was around as a child. Even though my horse was difficult to catch (all I caught her for was riding,) she knew when I was crying or just feeling down; because she was the first to greet me. My horse was faithful and trusted me everywhere we went. I have always been told I wouldn't amount to much or I wouldn't graduate high school. So because of this feeling, when someone says that an equine is worthless and won't amount to anything...I understand the horse and I believe they can amount to anything. I haven't read one wrong yet, and I hope I can always see value in them and people. I don't ever look at any obstacle or challenge as unobtainable; believe that they can do it!

As an example, I was ponying mares to another pasture. It was getting dark and I was using my husband's appaloosa gelding who has bucked him off every year he rode him. I took the gelding over when he bought his mule. My husband always told me to not to do things on him because he was unstable. I never listened and just did it. So I have two dominant mares on both sides of the appy gelding that are now going to a new pasture. Next, I am cantering back to the house to pick up more mares. Moving fast is also something that would fire up this appy gelding; he never even faltered and did it like he was a professional.

I remember, we went on a three-night four-day 40 mile ride to Bents Fort, Colorado dressed in pre 1840's attire and gear. Again, I rode the same appaloosa gelding, ponying a green-coming 3 yr. old john mule. My husband kept telling me to be safe and not to push things. The young mule pushed the appy into almost every cactus; the appy gelding had cactus needles all up and down his legs! We passed a rattlesnake that struck at the mule colt and they were both amazing! The worst thing on the ride was the last day after crossing the river, the young mule laid down with the pack on. These are a lot of examples of acceptance, trust, and believing in your livestock.

Forgiveness

I make mistakes while working with the equines and even if I have treated them wrongly, they still come to me for comfort and are willing to do the things I ask and go where I direct them. How many of us are that forgiving?

Patient

When I was the least patient, is when I have had the most problems. There is a communication barrier, and if you demand them into knowing what you are asking of them, immediately you will get bad results; but if you allow them to slowly understand, it will be rewarding lifelong.

Trust

On one of the occasions of riding, when I wasn't supposed to according to Mom; I'm pretty sure I got the ok from Dad, but Mom specifically asked me not to ride. My dad did graveyard shifts and would sleep during the day. So, I had to help watch my siblings during the day. Back to not riding when I wasn't supposed to...I was stopped by a friend that lived at the end of our road. He wanted to ride and I happened to be riding bareback. He insisted on riding in front. The bad thing about this is, my horse was difficult to ride bareback she had this way of rolling her body or turning sharply and causing you to fall off. I let him ride in front and as you probably guessed, we fell off. My horse took off and I tried catching her; she kicked me in the stomach. My mom was heading home at that time, and saw my horse running without a rider. I stopped at his house first to check my stomach where she kicked me and use the restroom. Apparently that's when my mom drove by. I learned that I shouldn't trust inexperienced riders. With all the equines I have trained or ridden I build a bond with them where they trust me and I trust them. I do not believe any of my equines would ever purposely hurt me.

I also remember, a two yr. old gelding owned by my ex-husband was started under saddle by me. On the second attempt to ride off the property, I really got to test his trust in me. I was less than one-quarter of a mile from his house and it was dusk. I saw a truck coming over one-half mile away. I was directing the gelding off the road into the ditch. With only the left hind hoof barely on the road, the truck passed. Apparently he didn't see us and missed my leg by one-half inch. After almost hitting us, the driver started swerving all over the road. Most reactions of equines is to jump or run off in those situations. This young gelding stood completely still. I could feel the tension in his body and I'm sure he felt mine as I braced to the worst.

Another example is after riding all day around the mountains, I would be tired and id fall asleep; my horse would take me all the way home safely.

This is kind of a trust/protection story my first paid training job was a horse named Dane. Through certain circumstances, I ended up with him temporarily. While walking in my hay pasture with my husband at the time, Dane apparently didn't trust or like him because he came in between us and pinned his ears at him. Every time he tried to get close he'd pin his ears.

Consequence/Reward

Watching the behaviors of the equine and how they socialize they are not to different from us. They both want to be around other horses, have a leader and have a friend. With that in mind, if one gets mad at one of the other equines, it's a rippling effect down to the lowest on the pecking order. The same is true in humans, so I chose to let it stop at me as much as I possibly could make it transpire. There is more pressure given when doing wrong things and less when doing the right things. This is true in our walk with God or just living out our days in school, work or just life. We tend to choose the wrong examples!

Focus

How much attention am I giving my equine? When I am totally focused, less problems arise and it's a very enjoyable ride. When my focus is elsewhere, that is when it becomes frustrating and dangerous. The same is true with our walk with God; we should be focused on our Lord. If you take the time to focus on the daily behaviors of humans/equines, you can learn a lot about them and can help them better.

Lead By Example

I am not lazy but I will take easier paths. One being ,let the seasoned equine train them. I say, work smarter not harder. They will learn so much faster following the older trained equine than what I can possibly show them. So obviously, putting the right equine with them is just as important to being around like-minded people. Putting someone who is a bad influence with our teens or children, is a bad idea. Surround yourselves and your families with good leaders.

Your Emotions Effects Everyone Around You

Your equine feeds off your emotion. If you are nervous/scared, then the horse will be nervous and scared. If you are hyper or anxious, then your equine is hyper and anxious. If you're dragging, your equine will react as the same. This is also true of being around people. Your behavior/emotions control those around you.

Philippians 2:14 [NIV] Do everything without grumbling or arguing,

You can control the environment around you by choosing to be joyful and offer forgiveness and humility. One act of kindness can change the world or your house.

Mercy

Even though I am a sinner and have done many horrible things God forgave me and gave me my family and amazing creatures, and land to call my home. When I am discouraged, I can watch a sunrise or sunset. I can sit in the wind and feel the breeze on my face and listen to it blowing through the trees. I can listen to rippling water in a creek or river. I can watch an equine run or play with the others in the herd. When sitting on their back, I'm amazed that such a mighty creature is humble enough to allow you to train and ride them. I feel free while on their back, as though I can go anywhere with them being free of judgement. God allows me to see the things I need to work on in my own life through my equines because I can see myself and I realize I cannot correct the behavior till I fix myself.

Fear

I have watched countless equines I have worked with develop trust in me to the point of even...though they are fearful they will still go through whatever I ask them to do. How willing are we to go through things God asks us to when we are afraid?

Are you afraid of what the future holds, afraid of losing everything, being alone, being judged... what is your fear? Can you put your complete trust in him even though you might fear?

How Can I Fear by Ron Hamilton.

When shadows fall and the night covers all; there are things that my eyes cannot see. I never fear, for the Saviour is near. My LORD abides with me!

How can I fear? Jesus is near! He ever watches over me! Worries all cease; He gives me peace. How can I fear with Jesus?

When I'm alone and I face the unknown; I fear what the future may be. I can depend on the strength of my Friend! He walks along with me.

How can I fear? Jesus is near! He ever watches over me! Worries all cease; He gives me peace. How can I fear with Jesus? Jesus is King! He controls everything! He is with me each night and each day. I trust my soul to the Saviour's control; He drives all fear away!

How can I fear? Jesus is near! He ever watches over me! Worries all cease; He gives me peace. How can I fear with Jesus?

Gratitude

What can you say you are grateful for? My list is now endless for things unseen and that I see. I used to live focused on the struggles, and now I find the positive and focus only on them.

You may think how does an equine show gratitude? How

do you show gratitude to others without using words? Maybe going above and beyond what would normally be expected in your job or activity. Fixing food for a friend and taking it to them or inviting them over. Giving them gifts, and so on. For an equine, it could be showing affection to you, being always willing to please you or being there, and offering an ear or something to lean on when you're down.

Chapter 8

Things I Learned About Myself Through My Equines

- When I'm stressed I can snap or react sharply.
- When overwhelmed I recluse.
- Very social.
- Calm.
- Trustworthy.
- Caring.
- Loving.
- Fun personality.
- Ornery.
- Stubborn.
- Curious.
- Loves to learn more.
- Seeking approval.
- Seeks fairness.
- Hates repetition.
- Protective.
- Loyal.
- Kind.
- Insecure at times.
- You have to earn my trust.
- Strong.
- Afraid of being alone.

- Irritable with things in my face or on my legs.
- Joyful.
- Loves challenges.
- Doesn't easily give up, strong willed.
- Senses pain or sorrow.
- Not an outcast.
- Not a failure.
- Me training was similar to raising my boys.
- I understood some of the feelings, God could have trying to teach me.
- I couldn't address the problems with my equine till I addressed my problem.
- I'll get back what I put in.

I started at an early age trying to bring joy into people's lives. While in Idaho, I rode to our friends house down the road. Their grandma was visiting, and she told me that she grew up on the back of a horse and she now missed it. I was able to get her on my horse and I led her on my horse. The grandmother was so happy she was crying; she told me she didn't think she was ever going to ride again. I figure, if I can add more smiles and joy in this hardened world, it would make everyone's life better. Because I know what it is like to have a dark and gloomy cloud hovering over one's self.

I know God has a plan for me that is greater than I could ever do on my own! So, I will go through my struggles with my head held high I will proclaim that he is going before me and fighting for me. I can say, I truly now have peace throughout the storms in my life.

Thank You

Thank you to my family for trying to understand me during my most difficult and challenging times in my life and for putting up with my issues. You have helped me grow and through your love and support, you led me in the right direction.

Thank you to God for being here and never giving up on me.

Thank you to everyone who has been involved in my life. Without any of you, this book wouldn't be possible.

Books Published By Every Cowgirl's Dream

- Answers To Your Mule Questions (A Common Sense Guide For New Mule Owners) by Cindy K Roberts
- The Mule Behavior Problem Solver -How Mules Think, Learn and React by Meredith Hodges, Steve Edwards, Chris French, Tim Doud, Red & Julie Wycoff
- How To Buy a Mule & Not Get Screwed—by Cindy K Roberts
- Life Lessons In the Saddle & Around the Manure Pile-Mule by Cindy K Roberts
- The Naked Truth About Mules & Donkeys—Myths, Legends, & Falsehoods Revealed by Cindy K Roberts
- Life Lesson's From A Rodeo Cowgirl—Taking Life By The Horns—A Tribute To Melissa Phillips World Champion Bull Rider by Melissa Phillips and Cindy K Roberts
- Mules, Coffee, & Oatmeal Cookies by Cindy K Roberts
- Run Pony Run by Stacie Smith
- The Performance Bred Saddle Mule by Cindy K Roberts
- The Lone Horseman by Larry Sarver
- The Lone Horseman II by Larry Sarver
- Eagle's View Horsemanship by Dennis Cappel
- Life Lesson's In the Saddle & Around the Manure Pile by Cindy K Roberts
- How to Overcome Negative Self-Talk: One Cowboy's Journey to Victory by Dennis Cappel
- Prairie Dust: Songs and Ballads from the Western Frontier by Burl L. Brooks
- Cinch Marks—Misadventures and Tall Tales From a Self Described Curmudgeon by Burl L. Brooks
- "According To Hoyle" A Dictionary of the Old West by Burl L. Brooks

- Training the Hard to Catch Mule by Cindy K Roberts
- Horse Sense Not So Common Tips by Burl L. Brooks
- Condemnation: One Cowboy's Victory Through Christ by Dennis Cappel
- Love Letters to Lillian by Cindy K Roberts
- Horse Trimming Made Simple by Dennis Cappel
- Confidence Training for the Western Saddle Mule by Cindy K Roberts
- Desperados of the Wagons West Expedition by Cindy K Roberts
- The Queen of Hearts is Your Best Bet by Cindy K Roberts
- Mule Shenanigans by Cindy K Roberts

WWW.EVERYCOWGIRLSDREAM.COM

LISTEN TO:

About The Author

Cassie Groff is a horse woman, mother, and devoted Christian that uses her horses and mules in a therapeutic horsemanship program to give support to those suffering from past emotional and physical abuse.

Believing that life is too short to be sad, mad or living a dull life, Cassie is a super active person that loves to play sports. Being an independent woman who loves history, Cassie's passions in life are fishing, camping, outdoor photography, swimming, boating, rafting, and thoroughly enjoys spending time in the mountains.

www.ingramcontent.com/pod-product-compliance
Lightning Source LLC
LaVergne TN
LVHW050344160826
845677LV00014B/3774

* 9 7 9 8 3 5 3 4 9 5 1 8 5 *